About t

The author, Ann Hudson, filled in time, waiting for the wind, when sailing in the Mediterranean, working on botanical illustrations, and went on to produce botanical illustrations of aquatic plants for Ness Botanic Gardens, University of Liverpool. The paintings were exhibited in Scotland where she was awarded the Royal Caledonian Horticultural Society Scientific Bronze Medal. This collection is held in the World Museum Liverpool.

Ann's illustrations of medicinal plants for Chelsea Physic Garden Florilegium Society are held in the archives.

A botanical illustration, *Ruta graveolens*, features in *The Illustrated College Herbal Plants* from the *Pharmacopoea Londinensis of 1618* for the Royal College of Physicians.

After concentrating on botanical collections, she returned to her passion, writing. It's in her blood; her grandfather was a newspaper editor.

Her son, Richard, at four years old, pleaded for a dinghy. He is now of a mature age and is a Laser 2000 sailing champion.

KISSED BY SUN AND WIND

Ann Hudson

KISSED BY SUN AND WIND

Vanguard Press

A CIP catalogue record for this title is
available from the British Library.

ISBN 978 1 784658 39 7

*Vanguard Press is an imprint of
Pegasus Elliot MacKenzie Publishers Ltd.*
www.pegasuspublishers.com

First Published in 2021

**Vanguard Press
Sheraton House Castle Park
Cambridge England**

Printed & Bound in Great Britain

Dedication

To Alan, my husband, who bought a catamaran sailing yacht.

To Richard, our son, who coped with early retired parents.

For Ian, our grandson, enjoy.

Donation to Royal National Lifeboat Institution.

Acknowledgements

RYA (Royal Yachting Association) for advice and assistance.

Bishop Skinner Marine Insurance.

KISSED BY SUN 'N' WIND

"Yes, I have lived!
Nor can an unkind fate
Take from me ever
The gifts of that former hour."

Attributed to Petronius

Preface

This is a memoir of a family pensioned off in the eighties, with a teenage son about to go up to university, who took the opportunity to change their lifestyle, to survive financially.

It highlights the contrast between the choice to cash in pensions in 2014-18, as traced against the history of Margaret Thatcher's England in the eighties: redundancies, early retirements and unemployment, and yet, a time of opportunities, venture.

There is a tide in the affairs of men, which, taken at the flood, leads onto fortune. (Shakespeare)

Set in Sardinia and Corsica, Mediterranean islands in the sun, it describes the flowers in spring, the festivals in February, the mountains and incredible fiord-like harbours and, above all, the many travellers met during explorations of these islands by the early retired who bought a boat and went where the boat took them; spending long periods lasting from three to six months at a time in France and Italy, sailing in the Mediterranean, becoming very well acquainted with the weather patterns, food and wine, and local people. It opens in Porto Cervo, the exotic port and village developed by the Aga Khan on the beautiful Costa Smeralda, where they "wintered over', having accepted the offer of a million pound pad to stay in.

We named our eight metre catamaran YB Yes... But, I said yes; Alan, my husband, said BUT...

Then he took over and at Easter 1983, with a skipper, together with the company of Richard, our son, and himself to crew the boat across the English Channel, en-route to Sardinia, Porto Cervo, to be berthed for cruising between Sardinia and Corsica, exploring the Islands in the Bonifacio Straits. They carried out searches for Santolina on the deserted islands for the University of Liverpool Ness Botanic Gardens. They sailed on across the Bonifacio Straits to Corsica, to explore the four star wonders of Corse, Bavella, Bonifacio and The Calanches, the fiord like harbours, and dramatic mountain passes with breath taking scenery.

The departure from Christchurch was advanced by twelve hours, as there was a depression coming into the Western Approaches and forecast for S E winds of 5/6 by mid-day on the Saturday, after a near calm night. They motored from Christchurch at 20.00hrs in a westerly wind easing to a force three. Visibility was very good and overcast clouds enabled them to see the reflected loom of the Barfleur light by 24.10hrs. The crossing was really uneventful.

The loom from the Casquets, Alderney, Barfleur, Portland Bill and St. Catherines could be seen for several hours, picking up the light on the western entrance of Cherbourg before dawn.

Our return journey home by ferry across the English Channel was very rough. The bar collapsed, fish and chips went flying; we had to hold onto our plates with a firm grip.

The car deck was chaos.

CAUTION always respect the sea.

SARDINIA

Part 1
1. Porto Cervo
2. Christmas & Wild Boars
3. Festivals
4. Powerboats – Sailing & Santolina

CORSICA

Part 2
1. Porto Vecchio
2. L'adventure Madame
3. Corsican people & French en route – Food
& Flowers
4. Wait for the Wind.

Chapter 1
Porto Cervo

Our rendezvous was Porto Cervo marina, Quay G, which was to feature in our lives for sometime, where we joined a small group of friends, helping and organising together the charter of their yachts. We did this to be able to be financially viable, to pay harbour dues and maintenance, plus enough to help with maintenance costs for Rich at University.

We had arranged to meet Mark, having received a letter back in England, the actual day we departed for Sardinia, telling us of a lovely villa he had found for us, if we would stay for several months. Our minds were in a turmoil, of should we? can we? why not? shall we?

"Good morning." Our thoughts were abruptly interrupted. "Good morning." We looked up into the blue eyes of a heavily built hunk of manhood, about five foot ten inches tall, of strong physique, with blond hair and a golden tan. "I am Mark. You are Alan and Ann. Come, I will show you the villa. Unfortunately I do not have the key with me, but I will show you the garden. It is a lovely garden. You like gardens, Ann? "

"Yes I love gardens." Someone had done some homework, much to my amusement, as I glanced across to my husband who was visibly groaning.

Mark continued, "Well, this garden is magnificent, you will like it. I lead you in my car a little way up the mountain." Mark waved vaguely in the direction of the hills densely covered in maquis.

Alan and I exchanged glances. "What the hell, we can always pull out." We returned to our car to follow Mark. We drove up the mountainside above Porto Cervo and turned slowly, almost up a dirt-track into the Via Brigantino. (The road of brigands.) Already we felt suspense, mystery, a slight uneasiness, which we brushed away as over imaginative. We came to a stop on a curving bend alongside a discreet looking villa.

Mark shut his car door and beckoned to us. "Come, we will go to the little casa first, I show you."

We went through the gateway, the entrance marked by two beautiful mimosa trees, opening onto a car park surrounded on two sides by vines, and then stepped onto a wooden veranda. I caught my breath as we stood gazing at the vista, the hills, the sea and immediately below, the harbour entrance, marked by the port and starboard buoys. The starboard light that beckons home! Mark watched my face carefully but feigned to ignore my presence as he talked to Alan. Alan was not seduced by all this beauty.

"Signora." Coming towards me was a gnarled old man, very bent, smiling, a delighted welcome all over his face. He gestured with hands towards the garden. I looked at Mark, who barely nodded, amused, as I followed the gardener into a bewitching fairyland. He indicated with glowing pride the new plantings of *Albicocchi,* a hosepipe snaked between the shrubs to water the new trees. He pointed to the lemons and oranges just forming into fruits. He crushed a spray of rosemary for me and held aside the sharp spikes of the variegated Agave americana overhanging the path, to let me pass amongst the euonymus and cupressus. My husband, with Mark, appeared by my side and, with a brief nod, the old gardener discreetly withdrew as Mark led on up some steps to the swimming pool. Leading off the pool were two sets of double French doors, beyond which one glimpsed a spacious, galleried, reception room, the furniture draped in dust sheets. To the side, a path between the conifers led to a small lawn, onto which double doors opened from the ensuite bedroom. We walked around the pool, the shadows of the Phoenix canariensis playing on the water, to the pillared terrace, furnished with marble tables and benches and hanging Italian pottery lanterns, and gazed out over the harbour. One breathed in deeply and felt one could stand here until the end of time.

Mark's voice interrupted the 'dreamy silence', a pregnant pause. "Come tomorrow, after lunch and the Steadmonds, the owners, will have arrived by then. They would like to meet you. At one o'clock." We nodded agreement and, as we took our leave, I noticed the gardener, smiling and nodding. I knew we would return.

We drove down the hillside to the marina to be greeted by Molly, "Well what have you two been doing to-day?" to which Alan replied, "Ann has been looking at gardens. Fatal!"

Molly chuckled. "Come aboard." Bob came up from below. Bob, who had been a Battle of Britain pilot, greeted us,

"Hello, you two, how's things?"

"Bad," said Alan. "Ann has been looking at gardens," and went on to say, "How do you like this? We are invited to meet the owners at lunchtime. They want us to stay for a few weeks to look after their swimming pool while Mark visits Canada."

Bob raised his eyebrows, "Well what's difficult about that? Just get the Ph value right." (The scientific measurement of alkaline to acid.)

Meanwhile, I told Molly about the beautiful villa and garden. The conversation took a general turn. Alan said, "Well, yes, it could give us time to refurbish and service our boat." It was a catamaran similar to Bob and Molly's although at this point the similarity ended. Their Snowgoose, fitted with electronics including radar, Decca, Loran C ADF, Navtex, Nautech 6000 auto pilot, a full set of Brookes and Gatehouse wind instruments, VHF and MF/SSB radios and log and depth instruments, not to mention the luxurious quality of the soft furnishings.

"If you arrange to do this, Alan, would you look after my boat as well?" asked Bob. "While we return to England?" he added.

"I'll let you know what we decide. See you later," responded Alan.

The following day, actually dressed in clean shore clothes and myself in dressy sandals with heels, a luxury after living in deck shoes, we drove back up the hillside, only to lose our way and, only with some difficulty, we retraced our path to the Via Brigantino, to find the white villa nestling into the hillside, this time noting the stone lions reclining inside the entrance. As we paused to take in the location and position of the villa and the adjoining little casa we realised that with binoculars we would be able to clearly see the catamaran moored on Quay G. Another plus point. The outer shutters in the vast entrance had been opened to reveal a large solid door and massive door bell-pull.

In a shaded corner seated at a small white table, slumped with head in hands, dozed the old gardener. We gently pulled the bell cord; the gardener didn't stir. The door opened promptly.

"Good-day, I am Carl." We were greeted by a tall, young to middle-aged, bronze Adonis of a man, with brilliant blue eyes and bright blond hair, almost too beautiful, with manners to match. "Come. Ah. Marie, here are the Hudsons."

"Ja, ja, ja. You like a drink no? I fetch a glass," said Marie, gathering up her sarong, as she padded barefoot into a magnificent kitchen. We sat, as most people do in Italy, at a long table on one of the large shady verandas, Marie is an enormous woman with a personality to match. She is in publishing and, as we were to learn, enjoyed a very comfortable, if not luxurious lifestyle. We exchanged small talk – the island, our families. Marie was saying, "We have two children. I call them children but, of course, they are grown-up now, thirty years of age, and when they come to stay with us, they have the little casa with the children. They make sand and mess. First, we have the little casa, then we have the villa. Carl and a pool. It is the most expensive swimming pool I have ever bought."

Marie's ample frame rippled, as she caught her sarong around her and said, "The swimming pool is essential here. It is so hot and we spend all our time around it."

"Come, Alan, I show you how to look after it, it takes only minutes." Carl went off below to the swimming pool with Alan into the small control room, leaving me with Marie. I turned her.

"The garden is very lovely, Marie."

"Ja, ja, zee garden. When you come, Ann, if you want lemons and oranges, you just pick what you want from the garden, and of course your children too must come to stay. Yes, yes, your family, that is important, and you can telephone them when you want." I felt tremendous relief, for I would be in touch all the time.

Carl and Alan came back onto the veranda. Mark looked up and exchanged glances with Carl. "Come Ann, I show you both the little casa. We go through the adjoining veranda, the back way."

The little casa was decorated in pastel shades and furnished with dusty pink sofas with covers and curtains in the natural goat wool, the hand-work of Sardinia. Absolutely beautiful work, very distinctive and expensive. A hand-made, off-white carpet covered the main reception area.

"So," said Carl, "if you can come, I let you stay here in the little casa, there is nothing to pay, as you look after my swimming pool. Just pay for the electricity you use and your telephone calls. Gas for the cooking is not necessary to pay, it comes with the casa. Good, we shall join the others."

"So that is that," said Carl.

Mark looked up. "Is it possible for you to be here by the 15th December latest, as I leave for Christmas in Germany before I go to Canada."

"Yes, it is possible. First we must return to England to make arrangements." Alan looked at me. "You realise, Ann, that it will be February before Mark returns and it is not a good journey to drive across the Continent then."

Carl said, "But you stay till spring and your children come for Christmas."

"Yes, yes." We all nodded, arrangements and reassurances agreed, and Marie handed me the key to the little casa, Casa Juanulloa.

Chapter 2
Christmas & Wild Boars

Christmas holidays on Sardinia last well into January. Very little stirs into life until the middle of the month. At the commencement of the festivities and through all the preparations leading up to Christmas Day, we discovered that our turkey dinner is not a tradition served on Sardinia. Instead, served lamb or veal is eaten. However the excellent supermarket, Sarma, in Porto Cervo produced three fresh turkeys, "For the English," and it really was superb, young and fresh. The plum puddings and the traditional fruit cake, which we have in England, were taken with us. The Sardinians eat panettone, a sponge cake streaked with chocolate, a large dome shape and rather disappointingly dry to our tastes. However, the Christmas tree was a little more difficult, as the island, surrounded by sea, being a salt laden atmosphere, is not at all sympathetic to the growth of our traditional Christmas tree. The salt stunts the growth and results in very poor, small, container grown specimens which are very expensive. We compromised with a delicate looking tree, natural to Sardinia. Sighs of relief, a traditional, family Christmas festival, as usual.

All was prepared and so we set off for the airport on Saturday morning, the capital town of Sardinia, some two hundred miles south, and would not arrive at the casa before brunch late on Sunday morning. We deliberately set out in daylight so that we could become au-fait with the route, returning at night, as the roads frequently deteriorate into narrow tracks across bridges, not always in a state of good repair. The halfway point was the only stopping place, with a garage and services for refuelling and a comfort stop.

Reaching Cagliari with time to spare we strolled round the old town and port, seat of the last kings of Sardinia, before continuing to the airport.

"Hi, Mum and Dad." Music to our ears and joy in our hearts as we sighted our son and daughter clearing customs. Hugs, kisses, mince pies and coffee, in that order.

"How far is the casa, Dad?"

"Some two hundred miles."

"Right, you've got yourself a relief driver."

We reached the casa, a very tired and happy family, but Richard, full of joie de vivre, cried, "This is great,' and with youthful enthusiasm was just about to jump over what appeared to him to be a low wall.

"No. Rich don't!" He stopped abruptly and looked over the little wall and he let out an oath, 'I could have broken my leg!" He discovered that the casa was built above and across great boulders in the hillside with a natural, cool cavern below. Marvellous for boat storage etc, but definitely not for jumping into!

Christmas Eve dawned, the first Christmas Eve, with little to do but choose what one wished.

"Let's go island hopping, or take the boat out?'

"Um, looks a bit doubtful weather-wise for the boat, besides we may not get back for Christmas Day."

"OK, island hopping it is then. We'll catch the ferry to Maddalena island and buy some wine and go 'stroll-about' and see what Christmas is like on Maddalena, the American base in the Italian Archipelago.

"Tonight, when we come back, we will go to the Pomadori, it'll give Mum the perfect treat, no work on Christmas Eve."

After a very full and perfect day we said our goodnights as we gazed out from the veranda and watched the light from the lighthouse flashing its warning signal. Within a couple of hours, the wind, the unmistakeable mistral wind, started to howl around the casa, followed by rumbling thunder. The storm struck.

We were awakened by Richard. "Dad, we have a problem. The Christmas tree is flashing and banging." "Don't be crazy."

"Seriously, Dad, there is a problem."

"Don't touch it."

"We haven't. Yes, of course its unplugged from the mains, as we always do at night-time."

Father dragged himself from bed, almost disbelieving. "A flashing Christmas tree. Umm, It must be caused by the storm."

"Yes, that's it, the lightning is bouncing from the wrought iron guard rail on the French windows and transforming flashes onto the tree baubles."

"Good heavens, it's your mother's flower

power. She has used florists wire to tie the baubles on the tree! Ann!"

All was forgiven on Christmas morning and the incident of the tree in the storm forgotten.

Walking down the hill to the Chiesa for the morning service, the wind was bitingly cold. The temperature had dropped to about six Celsius, very low for Sardinia; usually it is twelve celsius in winter.

The Chiesa Stella Maris is all white with a stumpy spire, 'the church of the bandaged thumb', as the family rudely christened it. Inside the walls are all white and the floor cool marble, with wooden moveable pews and kneeler benches. At Christmas time, the unusual feature that strikes the visitor is not one Christmas tree but three, perhaps to represent the Trinity. The trees are decorated with red poinsettias. In front of the altar is a tableau of the Virgin Mother, Joseph and baby Jesus, set on a raised bed of conifers surrounded by Euphorbia pulcherrima and tiny fairy lights. One gold pedestal of daisies enhances the setting, whilst the cross behind and high above the altar is adorned with enormous palms.

Families celebrate Christmas together, all over the world, where ever they may be. So, our family enjoyed a perfect Christmas Day, a Christmas to remember.

On Boxing Day the storm passed and the family were the only 'crazy English' to be sailing in the harbour, the traditional Boxing Day sail.

Porto Cervo, being a man-made village, enjoys, within walking distance, the church, supermarket including butcher, Post Office, bank, marina office, customs, yacht club, beach, garage, medical centre, stationery and newspapers, pharmacy, pub, garden centre, estate agent, hairdressers, the Sardinian craft shops and wonderful fashion boutiques from Rome, Milan, Paris. A continental showcase. Although the village is quite self-contained, the nearest market, and excellent indeed as the street markets are on Sardinia, is on a Wednesday at the nearest town, Arzachena, a half hour drive. A small town, one drives along the main route, hung with washing lines and rugs. Dirt track footpaths lead along the sides of the village dwellings. The atmosphere is friendly and busy, laden with the odours of freshly washed clothes and linen. The stalls of fruit and vegetables are piled high, including stalls displaying clothes, rugs and knitwear featuring beautiful Sardinian craft work. The market is patrolled by the market controller, looking after visitors. It is only worthwhile to drive into Arzachena and buy on market day in kilos, hence Wednesday morning became 'kilo humping'. So, on the Wednesday prior to Christmas week, we bought our fruit and vegetables, potatoes and pressimoli, parsley, not a curly variety as we know in England, but a spreading hand-span leaf, a little difficult to recognise at first.

Just as quickly as the temperature had dropped, it reverted back again to the usual average of twelve celsius as the wind magically died down, leaving all calm and so serene it was hard to believe the storm had happened. Before exploring the nearby beaches, we checked the security of the villa, as the storm had been strong enough to blow open the shutters and even the very large French doors leading onto the pool. The anxiety in this country when the mistral blows, for villa owners, are the wild boars. If they gain access they rampage through villa and garden, causing untold and costly damage, not least by making their homes for the winter on the premises.

On to the lovely small coves and beaches, white sand, crystal clear water. Our favourite, just ten minutes from the Casa, is Capriccioli, where one is enchanted by the beauty that entices one to stay forever.

After a wonderful day, arriving back at the Casa we were greeted by neighbours.

"Venite une festi." A party, at the villa just around the hillside. Everyone was delighted, the only reservations held by myself. Silently and frantically, I wondered how I could get out of it. In the end I simply said, "I do not wish to go because of the birds." I did send a gift with my apologies.

The couple renting the villa had worked in the Middle East and, having finished their Contract, were free to look around for somewhere to live and settle. Well, they arrived on Sardinia with all their belongings, books, hi-fi equipment, plus a dozen exotic speaking birds.

The birds were cold in Sardinia and made their dislike plain. So the largest bedroom, a suite in the villa, was provided for them at night time. After a few weeks of early mornings, the window frames had been pecked clean out and then they shrilled and screamed when the wind blew in. Imagine going to a party in that exotic company. Not for me. Far be it though that I deprive others of pleasure. The party was a huge success, with visitors from the Italian

Navy together with local people, rent a crowd, the norm for entertaining on a grand scale.

As it happened, Alan informed me that the birds turned their backs in disdain without moving or speaking and remained silent, heads turned watching on their perches. Perhaps just as nerve racking, for me.

So, the holiday for the family drew to a close and once more we set off for the night plane from Cagliary on January 4th, the last plane to leave the island until April. After heart-tearing farewells, Alan and I spent a couple hours until dawn under our duvet in the airport car park. We decided then to travel back up the west coast of Sardinia via Oristano. As we reached Oristano it was late morning, the sun was up and for the first time in 1987 we discarded our coats in hot sunshine. Along the coast road, the surf and spray made a spectacular display.

Everywhere, we saw dramatic posters in black and white advertising the coming festival within a few weeks, early in February. We decided to find out more and return to see the merrymaking. Continuing our drive back to the casa, I was horrified to be slowed down by a procession of cars with horns blasting out loudly. "Ann, for goodness sake pull over and stop."

"Gracious, whatever for?'

"Can't you see, a hunting party returning in triumph." I pulled over and stopped, quite, quite disgusted to see men hanging out of the car doors, wild boars, black fur, heavy snouts flattened onto the car bodywork, and their legs, spread-eagled and tied to the four corners of the car bonnets. Each boar had a bloody streak running down it.

The villagers all cheered but we did not stop long enough to see the distribution. Thankfully, we were ignored, as we had stopped our car in deference.

Alan had the final word, "It's food, Ann."

Chapter 3
Festivals

On a lovely sunny morning in mid January, at breakfast time, there was a soft knock on the door. Outside stood the old gardener, stooped low over a basket of oranges.

"Signora." He smiled, as he put the basket of oranges on the table and, with his pruning knife in his hand, he indicated towards the garden, inviting me to walk round it.

I was grateful for my weekly struggles with the Italian language lessons, so that I could understand key words, andiamo, let's go. Immediately outside the door to the veranda are the rows of vines and I wondered if Loe Mozzi, the gardener, intended to prune them. I strolled out with him, gesticulating with my hands towards the vines.

"No, in four weeks' time, early February. Today only, the ripe oranges are gathered so that these will not be damaged by wind." He responded in rapid Italian, gesticulating for me to understand. I opened up my notepad and pen and we strolled around the garden.

It appeared to be our day for visitors. At afternoon tea-time, a cheerful voice called in greeting, as Alan came around from the swimming pool with a lovely, youngish lady, beautifully groomed.

"I'm Chichi, I run Costa Service, and I have come to check on the villa after the storm. We check all the villas, but it may take us a few weeks, each storm, to get around all the villas." Over tea, Chichi explained Costa Service. "I service the villas ready for when the lady owners arrive for the season, to entertain company personnel and, in return, be entertained. The last thing they want to do is open their villa, spring clean, decorate and dryclean the soft furnishings. When we know the client is due to arrive, we move in with cleaners, electricians, decorators, gardeners, and we arrange the flowers in welcome. All is done, the deep freeze filled and we check all is working. In the meantime, we make periodic inspections, especially after a storm. Al'lora! you come to my villa and I cook spagehetti and vitello and pedistra for you."

So off we went and enjoyed a marvellous evening with another English speaking couple, also invited. At midnight, Chichi clapped her hands. "Now I go dancing! Venite!"

It was pouring with rain but already engines were roaring and off we all went in three cars. Down the coast road, brake lights flashing on every bend. This is madness. At last we all pulled in at what looked like a pizzeria. Inside many smiling faces, couples dancing old fashioned, country style waltzes, and at the far end of the barn, a roaring log fire, around which gathered all the members of families from teenagers to grandparents, all twirling forkfuls of pasta from pottery bowls. Chichi knew everyone and had a great time. We wondered about her and how such a lovely woman had come to live on the island, so alone and so beautiful.

Each morning, I would walk the few hundred yards down the hill to the Poste and check for mail, as most people do. However I was questioned at the Poste.

The postmaster said, "You are English, no?" I agreed. "In England, you have a postman, yes?" I again nodded in agreement. "So, in Sardinia, we send you postman." Well I was quite happy to walk to the Poste and collect any mail, but I nodded my thank you as courtesy demanded. Mystified, I walked back to the casa and reported to Alan that we were to have a postman and, within minutes, a car came up the hill, a postlady got out and delivered one letter. She knocked on the casa door, and in a torrent of Italian indicated, "Get a postbox."

"Io sono Anglaise, io non capito."

The reply came swiftly in English. "I am Italian and I don't understand!"

Alan was furious. "I will now have to get a box and somehow fix it onto a hard stone wall." Off we went to Arzachena to buy a post box and nails. With a little struggle and the spending of precious lira, we achieved a small metal box nailed to the stone entrance to the casa, with our name on it and keys. Poor Alan. He did not want yet another key to get his letters out of the box on the drive.

Marriage is, after all, 'give and take', so each morning I indulged at breakfast time the key to 'the post ceremony'. The other couple staying at a villa on the road around the hillside, he being American and she English, did not have a postman, most puzzling. No doubt all would be revealed in due course. In the meantime we asked questions, but to no avail. Knowing looks were exchanged, sophisticated worldly glances.

As Shrove Tuesday approached, we prepared to set off for a couple of days to tour the festivals at Christano and Bosca, places to which we had promised ourselves we would return. Earlier in the year, driving up the west coast from the airport at Cagliari, I managed to lose the village of Padria twice. Why, one wonders, did I want to find the little village of Padria, let alone miss finding it twice? This village led to the festivals. Clearly, on the long drives, exploring the length and breadth of the Island, the road to Padria was missed. It is easily done.

Approaching from the north or from the south on the one good fast road on Sardinia, the turning can be easily missed, but the little village is clearly signposted travelling from the town of Bosca, situated at one third of the way down the north west coast.

On the first Tuesday in March, very early in the morning, we set out to visit the festival at Bosca. Travelling south the weather was not unpleasant, with a temperature of fifteen Celsius and the wind blowing from the north west, but overcast with cloud. At this time of the year, the island celebrates, with carnivals lasting over five days of holiday. The Sards have an immense amount of ability for pure self enjoyment, casual, simple, fun-loving, pure freedom. The carnivals are just for this purpose and do not combine with efforts for raising funds for charity, hospitals or lifeboats. They claim there is no need as all is provided and they have sufficient for their needs. We drove into Bosca and parked near the river for a coffee stop prior to exploring the old town. The atmosphere in Bosca is Spanish; the central thoroughfare is an example of town planning inspired by Aragon.

On festival day, the inhabitants promenade in the streets in the morning, all dressed in black. The young boys, carrying dolls, call on the housewives, asking for milk. In the evening, the villagers parade, all dressed in white, proclaiming that milk has been provided. The harvest is assured. Much merriment and amusement, noise and laughter and singing is created in the narrow old streets. During the siesta, being mad English, we climbed up the steep path to the castle Serravalle. After that, the decision was taken not to wait for the late evening procession in the town. Already the noise from the funfairs could be heard and so, much amused and relaxed we started on the long drive, some hundred odd miles, back to the Costa Smeralda. On leaving Bosca, one more try was made to locate Padria, and there was the signpost, the narrow road winding up the hillside. A quick look at the time, why not, we thought, and turned the car up the hillside road.

The joy of finding a peaceful rural village in a picturesque, tranquil setting. The village square, shaded by a few very old trees, the monument listing all the names of the men who gave their lives for Italy during the two world wars. In the early evening, people were gathering on the village square. We parked in a side street and strolled among the villagers. We were beckoned from across the square.

Under the trees, friendly Italian voices called to us, indicating that they wished us to drink with them. Ah, we thought, festi, accepting graciously and admiring the wine. "Molto bene, grazia."

We were joined by another man, speaking rapidly in French. "Vous êtes Français?" he asked and, without waiting for a reply, continued to speak very quickly in French, gesticulating and drawing us towards a building with closed shutters. "Parlez vous lentement, s'il vous plaît." Then we understood that he was inviting us into the building. "Mais oui," he beckoned impatiently. A trifle dubious, we followed.

Up went the shutters and we found ourselves in a concrete shell of a building, with a massive long table, covered with a snowy white cloth, on which stood baskets of fritella, small doughnuts, beautifully lightpuffs of pastry, dusted with icing sugar, and baskets of fresh figs and much, much wine. The glasses were quickly replenished and we soon realised to sip very slowly, the wine appeared to be limitless and in very generous supply. Local Italians gathered round, smiling, raising glasses in greeting and we were asked if we like the wine. Clearly, they were very proud of it. Of the two varieties of wine, one clear, bright and fruity, obviously their best produce.

At this point, as we continued to communicate with our limited knowledge of Italian and French, an English voice was heard. "Good evening, you are English? Yes. I am Tonio. Please enjoy yourselves." BBC English, sweet music to our ears and much relief from the constant strain of foreign tongues. We quickly realised that we were being addressed by the host, as the Italians called him Boss. He invited us to partake of the buffet and to stay and enjoy ourselves and join in the dancing. Once again, we accepted graciously honoured to be allowed to join in such a delightful occasion. First, more wine, then we tasted the fritella, light and melting in the mouth. Fritella, to us is similar to a very light and delicate small doughnut. It is the Sardinian word for pancake. We then tried the various puffs of sugared pastry, so light it melted on the tongue and yet more wine.

We asked our host if they had a collection for the local hospital.

"No, no, it is not necessary, I provide everything for the festi for the people of my village and we are delighted to welcome English people." He went on to explain to us that the building shell in which we stood would soon be completed and he would open a pizzeria, the only one in the village, indeed the only one in the four surrounding villages. We talked about food and he explained that he only wished to do pizza as it is what is wanted and besides, he did not wish to have the bother of meat. In Sardinia, the pigs are used for ham only, raw or cooked, and by English standards it is very expensive. The rest of the pig is used up in salami.

Music is heard. The band has arrived and they set up a dais made in the square. From side streets appear donkeys, bearing their child riders wearing national dress in colours of red, black and white. Dusk falls as the procession parades, children dance around the maypole and an effigy of King George is hosted high above the heads of the crowd. All the villagers then partake of the food. The baskets are passed joyfully amongst the villagers, glasses are filled, a truly family occasion. When all is tidied up, the villagers join hands and form chains to dance in weaving patterns to a steady one-two-three rhythm on the square. Others reach for the ribbons of the maypole. Enchanted, we join in and very quickly pick up the step as we are guided by our hosts. Cheeks glowing, the music stops. Our English speaking host, Tonio, joins us. He is anxious that we have a hundred mile drive back to the Costa Smeralda, but we assure him not to worry as we are used to driving on long journeys.

"Next time, when you return, we will have a room for you to stay," he tells us. We thank him and taking our leave, ask him where he learnt fluent English. His answer– "But London, of course, wonderful, wonderful London. There I have a super time but now I return to my village in Sardinia and open a pizzeria for my mother, who is eighty one years of age and for my people. I was the head waiter in the Savoy Hotel, London."

CHAPTER 4
Powerboats – Sailing and Santolina

As we prepared to sail, Mark strolled up the quay and we passed the time of day over a cup of coffee. The Canadian visit was still fresh in Mark's memory and he gave a glowing account of celebrating Christmas with his family and friends in Canada.

Well, we are off around the islands for a day or two, up to Spargi and Budelli, stopping at Maddelena, a favourite with the visitors and tourists. Usually on the quayside, American personnel stroll and are always helpful, in calling to take our mooring line and to fasten on the quayside. However, on one occasion a very large yacht flying the Amerian flag made it very tight to moor up on the quay.

Alan hailed the yacht. "Hi America, please move over for us to moor on the quay."

The American skipper manoeuvred the position.

Later that evening at G&T time, we enjoyed a drink with the American skipper and his wife. He explained that they had sailed from Miami across the Atlantic ocean, but the difficulty, he explained, was 'parking' the yacht.

Visiting friends in the port later, they informed us the large American yacht sailed in with much barging and calling, before managing to moor up.

The American couple of a mature age and delightful company, told us they were on their way to gay Paris to winter over, as they had received and opened their post in the port, only to read and be told by their family, it was time for them to settle down, and the family had purchased for them a condominium in Miami. As they explained they were much more concerned with the thought of settling in a condominium than sailing across the Atlantic Ocean and were making haste to winter over in Paris.

The weather forecast for the next day or so is belle encore, my sort of weather. All too frequently the weather in the Mediterranean can be unstable and we constantly study the weather patterns, watching for the dreaded m'auviso, gale warning, with winds up to force seven and over. A frequent phrase is 'temporale con locale colpi di vento,' thunderstorms with gale force gusts locally.

An interesting feature on some of the headlands, or sometimes overlooking a small cove, are the watchtowers, still very much in evidence, which were built to warn and protect villagers or shipping in the anchorage against the depredations of Barbary pirates, and many were still manned even after Nelson's time. Today, these serve as very useful landmarks.

In May the islands are a sheer delight, carpeted with dwarf flowers, yellow, red and blue poppies, flax and Santolinas. The silver grey foliaged Santolina was of particular interest, as we had promised to search out and locate the native Santolina on the Italian islands, as this plant appears to have a cloning peculiarity. We had the most interesting time, taking the dinghy ashore and searching. Frequently, we found what we thought was Santolina, only to find on close examination the required features were not exactly true. Whilst it was interesting, it was at times most frustrating as so many of the grey foliage plants are similar.

As the islands are frequently quite deserted, our presence disturbed the birds; our climbing high up the hillsides resulted in the larger birds, becoming agitated, swooping down, screaming at us. Naturally, this behaviour hampered and limited somewhat our search area. But, we finally achieved our object, or at least Alan did, and carefully we noted the location, date and took photographs. Our findings were passed to a scientist at the University of Liverpool Botanic Gardens at Ness, for a paper being written on Santolinas, including those found on Sardinia. Satisfied that we had indeed located, in the wild, the Santolina for which we searched we turned our attention to the next island to explore: Corsica, a beautiful, natural island of forests and mountains. With the weather settled, we decided to sail on across the Bonifacio Straits. Reaching Santa Manza Bay and onto Rondinara, we realised we had sailed off our charts and that we needed the next chart, into Porto Vecchio. So although we really did not like sailing without the chart we decided we were so near and could not be far off La Chiappa lighthouse, marking the channel. I resolved at the first opportunity to purchase the required chart.

Although we had briefly visited Porto Vecchio previously, we did not have time to explore it thoroughly, so we planned to put this right and arranged to 'winter over' the boat at Porto Vecchio and to return in the Spring. We sailed back to Porto Cervo first for the World Cup Powerboat racing in June 1988. So, up betimes at five-thirty a.m. to set sail once again. The wind was with us and we anticipated by five p.m. we would be moored up back on quay G. Not quite! The seas on the Maddelana Archipelago became too heavy and we returned to spend the night at Palau, hoping to reach Cervo the following day. After a welcome lunch and siesta, on arriving back on our mooring, we telephoned our friends, Noami and Lionel.

"Hello, Alan and Ann, calling."

"Where are you?" came the rapid response.

"Moored up on quay G in the marina here in Porto Cervo."

"Great, we will come at once." They were delighted to be on board and, with the promise of the power boat racing on the next day, with the hope and excitement of trying to photograph power boats at speed, plans were made in anticipation of a beautiful, calm, bright, perfect morning.

We were lucky indeed. The morning dawned, just perfect. Norma and Lionel arrived exactly on time for a nine a.m. start, hurrying along the quay, complete with cameras.

"Good morning," Alan called, "we are ready to slip our mooring. When we are out of the marina, would you like to take the wheel, Lionel?"

Naomi interrupted, "He's never done that."

"Ssh," admonished Lionel.

Her eyes widened and she asked, "Can you do it? Will we be safe?"

No time for questions, as we neared the port buoy at the harbour entrance, along with the massive French and Italian cruisers. We, but a tiny eight metre catamaran. Off we sailed, to a position well behind the start line, as the power boats roared past us in a cloud of spray. It was so exhilarating that even I forgot to be frightened. We slowed our engine and stood off the start line, cameras at the ready. Lionel and myself, the photographers, sat up on the bow and as Lionel dangled his feet overboard between the hulls in an effort to catch the right shot, he called to me.

Tell the skipper to hold her steady, he's wetting my feet."

Lined up on the start, the French entry, Rocky, then the British entry, Reporter. On the finish line on the Friday, first place went to the Italian entry, Cesa, much to their surprise and delight. Word was that this boat had not performed at all well and the entry from GB, Reporter, was tipped hot favourite, only to develop engine problems and retire. A new engine arrived that day and the crew worked around the clock to overcome their disappointment.

Luchaire second, Italy Gancia Dei Gancia fourth, Italy Barbero third, Italy Honeywell fifth, Italy Miura sixth, Italy. An Italian Triumph.

We understood Reporter did overcome her engine problems. The power boats flashed past us on both port and starboard bows, tremendously exciting.

Lionel declared he had never had such a breathtaking experience.

After the race, the half dozen spectator boats, including ourselves, sailed back into Porto Cervo harbour, round the starboard buoy, ourselves to anchor off in the bay for lunch, which was prepared on the 'finish line' as we swung up and down. The salad was well washed. Ham, dolcelotti with black grapes, fresh tomatoes in olive oil and basil, enjoyed with with a bottle of Chianti Classico.

After a long siesta, we motored back to our mooring on Quay G. That evening we dined on the veranda of the superb villa in which Lionel and Naomi were the guest of the Vermouth company. Before dinner, we strolled through the garden onto the quay to chat with the crews of the various entries in the power race. Fortunately, some of the mechanics were British.

So, the day ended as the sun set over Porto Cervo.

Returning to the little casa, tired, that pleasant exhaustion after a perfect day, rare indeed, we met up with the Steadmonds and shared a nightcap. The conversation took a turn, "Ah, yes, well, the letter box." They exchanged glances. "On Sardinia, many people come, they fall in love and in love with the island. They buy very, very expensive real estate and then boom! Problems. They separate, it causes many problems, many heart breaks. But you are British, you do not have these problems. The sun here is hot, the scenery exotic, it is, you know, corrupt, seductive." We listened, we sympathised, but we were hardly flattered. So much for the great British reserve. Hardly flattering, or is it highly complimentary?

The final joke was on me. After we had left the island, a letter was posted to me from the little casa, from a friend, in an envelope sealed with a picture of ripe cherries.

The following morning, Alan called from the garden in great excitement. "Ann, come and look."

Well, there in the garden was the most enormous tortoise, as big as a bowler hat. Alan ran into the kitchen for bread and milk. He was delighted. Alora! as the Italians say. We went down to the boat and started preparations, stocking up, provisioning etc, things to take with us to move the boat up to Corsica. Alongside, in the berth but one, was a very impressive and expensive motor yacht. The skipper waved a welcome and as we busied ourselves onboard, he stood and watched. Alan went off up the quay, leaving me onboard. It was near coffee time – eleven a.m. The skipper on the motor yacht called in greeting and offered morning coffee.

I hesitated, but then thought, why not? A beautiful morning and, adjacent on its berth, a beautiful yacht. Over coffee, the skipper introduced himself as Gino and said he was a 'deep sea Master' en route for his ship moored at Livorno. He asked where we were bound in the 'fun-tub'

"To Corsica," I answered. His face immediately clouded over.

"No, Ann, you must wait, you cannot sail to Corsica until Thursday, maybe later, you will not get up the east coast of Corsica for some days. Look at the weather, Ann. You will have drinks with me tonight."

"Perhaps, I see." Rather anxious, I was keen to get away from magnetic Gino and back onto the everyday fun-tub Y.B.

When Alan returned, he just dismissed it from his mind, unimportant. Later that evening, Alan met one of his harbour companions and off they went for a chat and drink. So, immediately, Gino was on the deck, calling, "Ann, Ann!" He stood there, hands on hips, commanding,

"Ann, I want you, I have you!" Good gracious do I use polite reason? "Ann, I take you to Florence and Rome." I started to panic. In the Mediterranean, one moment it is light, the next darkness has fallen. Really, this is crazy. "Ann, come I have you."

I moved quietly, hardly daring to breath as I locked the cabin door. Dear God, Alan where the hell are you. I don't want to see Florence and Rome or go round the world. I've seen Florence and Rome and the world will still be there. This guy is magnetic! I heard him breathing heavily on the deck, my deck, and I stood absolutely still inside the cabin with lights not switched on.

"Ann, are you awake?" Thank God, Alan. I was furious! Alan roared with laughter. "What, you are joking, you've gone to seed, love."

The next morning Gino stood, hands on hips on his deck, staring at me. Alan started to go to the showers on the quay with his towel and shaving gear, met Gino, eye to eye, realized the guy had his engine running and could slip his mooring before he, Alan, could get out of the shower. Alan changed his mind, came back on board, threw his toilet gear on the pilot berth, started the engine, and slipped our mooring, before Angelo had figured that we would be away before him. Gino had meant business; kidnappings do happen. He wanted a galley slave!

We sailed out of Porto Cervo for Palau. At the gulf of Arzachena the seas swelled up into a heavy roll, almost too much for us. Alan looked at the chart and decided to heave to in a little bay, unknown to us. Another boat lay at anchor. Suddenly frantic waving from the other boat, then a horrid grinding noise, reverse engine fast. Oh no, the engine labouring! It's free! Rather white faced, we realised, despite our low draught the bay was not suitable.

Nothing for it but to sail on to Palau, in increasing seas. After an uncomfortable hour we thankfully reached Palau and moored up. How well I remember Gino's words, "You must wait Ann." How right he proved to be. Sweet fate, Gino or the sea?

Several days later, exhausted and very tired we reached Porto Vecchio, moored up on the visitors' quay and slept for twelve hours. The next day we met the harbour master and chatted about England, Cheshire cheese and Corsica. We were invited to moor Y…B, our island fun tub, on the residents' quay and become residents of Corsica. A pleasure and delight for us, enabling us to explore this beautiful island and sample the food and wine.

PART 2
CORSICA

Chapter 1
PORTO VECCHIO

Brooding, solemn, enticingly beautiful Corsica, an island very hard to leave.

"I had got upon a rock in Corsica and jumped into the middle of life." Boswell.

When we first sighted Corsica, parts of the coastline looked as if it had been formed by a giant in a rampant rage hurling rocks at the land. Just a little daunting, steering the boat well clear, we continued on to La Chiappa point, the coastline softening into enormous, rounded, upturned-pudding-shaped hills. These features are so distinctive, one can immediately recognise one's position. We nicknamed the island – the land of the puddings.

Our mooring in Porto Vecchio is very protected within this large sheltered inlet, in a magnificent mountainous setting, lying close under the old Corsican town. It has been praised since the earliest times. Boswell wrote that *'Porto Vecchio may vie with the most distinguished harbour in Europe'.* Sailing directions of Nelson's day described the harbour as being *'The best in the island, also one of the finest ports in the Mediterranean'.* It is reached after sailing up a very long channel, a channel with delightful sandy coves and little private bays, inviting and beckoning on both sides. The picturesque old French town of Porto Vecchio is situated dramatically above the Port; to reach it is a steep climb up to the walls and one enters by the enormous 'Porte de feu' set within the walls, which are several yards in width. The stone is creamy yellow mixed with granite. The side streets are full of restaurants, likewise the square, where delightful festivals are held. Using the church as a backdrop, the cafés with brightly coloured striped awnings surround it to form a natural, cobbled and slab paved stone stage on which the local dancing school perform formation ballet to a very high standard.

Besides all the restaurants are some splendid boutiques displaying unmistakeably French clothes, yes, expensive. One superb shop is the L'Orriu, Old Cheese, liqueurs, wines and herbs. All the goodies are beautifully displayed in baskets, bread, herbs, wild boar pâté, blackbird pâté and myrtle liqueur, the odours mingling with the smell of the enormous cheese displays of roquefort, goat, chevre, brie, amongst a numerous variety.

We did our shopping, a little cheese to spoil ourselves, a little pâté, some delicious bread, a flute and a margarite. A visit to the bank and the Post Office and set off walking back down the hillside to the port, passing the Cave Vin Directe, on the way. This 'off licence' is in a garage run by a family. Monsieur, beaming and smiling, offers his wine. Large carafes of it grace the tables on most of the yachts visiting the port.

Down to the port and back on our mooring, we are greeted with, "Hi! I'm Emma, you must be Alan and Ann." The amazing point about sailing, yachts and ports is the friendly companionship, especially to fellow countrymen abroad. The British flag is an entrée to the social life. "That's right, we are Alan and Ann and we have just moored up. We are looking forward to exploring Corsica."

"Ah yes, it is beautiful. Do you have a car here as well?"

"Yes," we respond.

"Well, you can go up into the mountains, to Bavella Pass and L'Ospedale lake. Now, I am collecting my post, we meet again, we are moored along the quay. We are busy now but soon, in a few days, you come for drinks. Goodbye for now."

Nodding farewell, we looked forward to making further acquaintance.

Each day at the Port de Plaisance, the weather forecast is displayed and, of course, it is a meeting place for discussion as naturally, everybody checks the latest weather forecasts from Nice. The harbour master, Monsieur Lesguer is extremely efficient at posting up the daily forecast and special bulletins or gale warnings, mistrals which can last for five to nine days.

Strolling along the quay to check the forecast, we were greeted by, "Well, we are not going anywhere today." A tall thin man with a beard, and dressed in formal navy trousers with a marine type jersey, carrying a folder, made this very positive announcement. Puzzled, we looked at the forecast. Still puzzled, we listened to his next comment, addressed to us. "No, diesel. Do you happen to have some diesel or know where I can get some?" We groaned. Of course, the 'en grieve' fuel strike, including the harbour.

"No, sorry. Only yesterday we actually gave some ten gallons away! A return favour, fuel we had filled in one of our tanks in error whilst not paying close attention during the excitement of the powerboat racing.

The stranger introduced himself. "I'm Robin. I'm here for just a month, updating the South of France Pilot. I aimed to sail around the island, but in the time it will not be possible. Good sailing," and with a wave of his hand he hurried off up the quay.

So for the next few days we decided to conserve our fuel, both in the boat and car, planning only to explore the outskirts of Porto Vecchio. The first thing we did, of course, was to obtain the Michelin map. I resolved to find an English printed guide book. This I did after trailing around the town and finding two 'papier librairie' (newspapers and magazines) and further along the quay a ships chandler. I then looked in at the ships chandler and to my delight I found, in my size, white leather deck shoes by Du Barry, which feature a red triangle inserted into the outside of the left shoe and a green triangle of leather into the side of the right shoe. Port on the left, starboard on the right. Being able to glance quickly at either foot was most reassuring following instructions whilst taking the helm. Port left hand down, starboard right hand down.

However, to find a guide printed in English, I had to search the bottom shelves and, finally, tracked down a beautiful coffee table book with excellent photography. So good, it immediately inspired us to go and see the 'wonders of Corse'. Bavella Pass and maybe by boat to the Calanches, but certainly to Bonifacio.

The lifestyle in the Mediterranean is very leisurely, or is it just as tiring? In many ways, more fulfilling as the day is, separated into two equal parts sandwiched with a couple of hours siesta. One does adjust to the climate, almost, as one is only too aware of the Mediterranean sun and the sexual hunger it provokes; the very elements claw at one's physical being, screaming for fulfilment of the flesh. The human sickening realization that this could actually happen to one, demands enormous self-discipline. So easy, so many attractive guys only too willing for a 'quick roll around the hull' This is reality.

One searches and thankfully finds 'douceur de vivre' in the exquisite little bays, deserted, golden sand, aqua crystal water; all to be enjoyed along with the natural products, the fruits and the vegetables, the salads, and above all the wine.

Siesta over for another day, more chores, load the laundry into the ship's laundry box, a rectangular plastic box with cut-out handles for carrying and tying on deck. Everything, but everything including oneself at times, on a yacht is secured. Back up via the gentle slope to the old town to find the 'laverie' and work out how to operate it. While I stood, absorbed in this menial task, a wonderful voice behind me said, "Excuse me, ma'm, do you understand the number of these programmes?" Startled, I looked into the twinkling eyes of a well-built, healthy youngster, just like my own son. "Well, I think so," I replied.

"Which programme is right for slacks like these?"

"Oh, I would say four or five drip dry synthetic."

"Oh, gee whizz, ma'am, I chose programme one and now I have boiled my pants?"

Bless him, I could have put my arms around him. He grinned and as quick as lightning changed the programme number to four. The pants survived.

"Tell me, ma'am, I'm touring this country on foot, what's it like?"

I tried to describe Corsica, what little I had seen.

"Gee ma'm I guess this is going to be energetic. Have you been to my country, British Columbria?"

"Why no, but I would love to, maybe some day."

"You really must, ma'm, it's very beautiful, a magnificence and grandeur all its own. I love it, ma'am, I grew up in the mountains, running free in wonderful fresh, clear air. Have a good trip, ma'm."

Laundry has never been such a pleasure.

Back on the quay, it's time to drive out to the hypermarkets, a household garden centre with just everything from wallpaper and paint to luxury garden furniture. On the opposite side an industrial site with Yamaha and Riva, a hospital. All within a half hour drive of an airport not to mention the little ferry port adjacent to the harbour, plying tourist routes to the mainland, across the Bonifacio Straits to the Italian Archipalego and mainland Italy. Strangely enough, or perhaps not so strange, on the southern side nearest to Bonifacio, is an Italian hypermarket and on the northern side of the town, the hypermarkets are both French. Usually the French end wins, as the hypermarket boasts fashion and shoe boutiques; in fact, almost everything under one roof.

Returning to Y.B. a note has been pinned up. *Come for drinks nine p.m. Emma. Yacht Ornsay.* In the cool of the evening we strolled around the quay to find Ornsay, unmistakeably a steel hull, Clyde motor yacht built in the inter-war years and, as we were to learn, used for coastal defence during the last world war. Going below into a spacious salon, Emma greeted us. The salon was on two levels and was rather like walking into a comfortable world back in the 1920s. The high level nearest the deck was carpeted, comfy chairs, navigation charts, books, paintings; whilst below, the wooded floor is luxuriously covered with rugs; again comfy sitting room chairs, photos, books and more books, plants and a wonderful coffee table made from a ship's wheel.

Emma, all five foot of her, slim and glowing with good health, pushing back a strand of long blond hair, explained. "This is my house, Ann, so it has all the things I would have if I lived in a house. A really good galley in which I can cook almost anything."

My glance strayed to a book shelf in the galley and caught sight of "Entertaining with John Tovey'

"Ciao a cara."

"Ah, here comes Giorgio," and Emma introduced her husband. Giorgio explained that he had been working on his boat on the next berth, the "San Giuseppi'.

"I go first to have shower, excuse me."

"The 'San Guiseppi'is our working boat," explained Emma, it belongs to a company in which I am a director.

Giorgio manages it and we live on my yacht, 'Ornsay'. Giorgio will show you around the 'San Guiseppi'. She was used, you know, by the Italian Government for research in the Antarctic, for which Giorgio led the team. The San Guiseppi is a wooden hulled barque, built over strength to take Antarctic ice.

"Oh yes," continued Emma, "barque rigged with long range diesel and full traditional rigging including tan cotton sails. Yes, she's beautiful, but very hard and often dirty work to maintain. We use her now for tourist trips. The tourists find her fascinating and love to actually sail her to the Italian archipelago, Maddelena, for lunch and shopping." As Emma talked Giorgio returned.

"Forgive me, cara, always there is much to do. Now, Alan and Ann, what can I offer you? Ah, Emma has looked after you, but a 'top-up' yes? G&T is the favourite everywhere I think, no?"

The men chatted and inevitably exchanged views over the war; Giorgio, high ranking in the Italian Army. He shakes his head. Alan, a Captain in the British Army seconded to the Indian Army in Mountbatten's headquarters. "But come, Alan, I show you San Guiseppi, no more war, and off went the men.

"Would you like to see Ornsay, Ann?" The cabins were equally as spacious and comfortable as the salon and, of course, three or four heads with showers, one for each cabin. "These are cabins for my children. I have a son and daughter, grown up now and away at university but they come and see us in the vacations and they keep some of their books and records, musical instruments and bikes on board. My daughter's cabin is stuffed with cuddly toys collected from all over the world.

Their father and me were in ship broking. We bought and sold ships and lived on whatever ship we had at the time." Emma wandered around reminiscing. "It was so romantic, I met him in Spain, I was bored on hols and he said, "Come to Japan with me." We spent every minute together, travelling and buying and selling boats, and then he died. Fortunately for me he had put all the boats in my name, but I found myself in some remote part of the world with two small children and I needed to sail to England and the only boat sailing was the San Guiseppi so I hitched a lift with the captain. That is how I met Giorgio and I have been by his side ever since."

"How exciting and how romantic!" I remarked, almost lost for words, in the company of such an amazing woman.

"Ah yes, it was, although my first husband was eighteen years older than me. Giorgio and I married in a little village church in Portugal, near Villamura, not a civil marriage, a church wedding, because of Italian laws. It is best for me to live on my boat under a British flag."

Chapter 2
L'AVENTURE, MADAME

On a lovely sunny morning in May, we set off with a picnic for the lakes and mountains.

Quickly our route led us out of the town, the road narrowed and we started to climb, gradually. Soon, the road wound round and round upwards, narrowing, becoming more like a very wide path in a giant rock garden. Bordering the pathway, pine trees, broom, cork trees, olives, arbutum, and mustard, growing rapidly day by day, the enormous Corsican hellebores, colourful cyclamen spreading a carpet beneath the trees. The air was cool and sweet, perfumed by the vegetation and the undergrowth of the maquis, growing luxuriantly as far as the eye could see. The mountain road wound up to Bavella. Turning a bend, we came upon a wonderful sight, a large, cool, aqua blue lake in a setting of pine trees. Along the shoreline snuffled families of pigs, goats and cows roaming at random. L'Ospedale Lake, a calm, serene oasis. A French family picnicked by the waters edge, the men fishing. Perfect tranquillity, providing a lunch stop, leaving us spellbound with its magic. A place we returned to time and time again, never to be able to drink in sufficient of its beauty.

But, onto more delights, the road continues through the rock garden to level out at the top of the Pass, high in the mountains of Bavella, a natural, majestic grandeur beyond imagination. It just took our breath away, gazing in wonder and awe. Through the pass, one follows the road which descends gradually back down to the coastline, pausing only for the families of wild boars occasionally blocking the path.

Returning back at Porto Vecchio harbour, a man approached us, smiling, although obviously stiff down one side of his body as he walked hobbling along, using one side of his body more than the other.

His attractive eyes twinkled in greeting. "Alan, have you by any chance a drill with you?"

"Yes, I have, by all means borrow it. Come aboard. Larry, meet my wife, Ann."

We exchanged greetings, while Alan went to find the drill. "I am working on my boat, it needs a great deal of work in preparation before we sail for Mombasa, we will sail via the Red Sea."

"Why Africa, why the Red Sea?"

"L'aventure, Madam, and I love Africa. I work for the World Health Organisation from time to time. Ah, thanks, Alan, my own drill will be back tomorrow after repair." On Larry's departure I asked Alan, "Where did you meet him?"

"Oh, in the capitainerie, shaving one morning."

"What does he do?"

"Well he works, as he says, for the World Health Organisation from time to time, but I rather think he is a pilot. Why not ask him to dinner? He is all alone and may appreciate it."

"OK When he returns the drill, I will invite him."

"Ann, it is a perfect evening, let's slip our mooring and go round to San Cyprianu and anchor for the night, dine when we get there." We motored up the channel, put up the sails, and arrived around in the next bay within a few hours, pleasantly tired. Tucked well into the small bay, we anchored in the perfect still of late evening. The fish quickly came around the boat looking for food. Over the stern, the British flag drooped, a slight flutter stirred it into life, then utter stillness. The sea calm, almost mirror- like, the surface shaded by slight movement. Nearer to the rocks, the water held in the still depths reflections of dark aquamarine on the port bow, interspersed by a deep narrow reflection of cerise from the dark red jagged rocks, and deep on the starboard bow, lime green from the mustard plants. The hills brooding, heavy, shaped like turned-out puddings, revealing sharp outlines against the twilight, as a dense mist slowly rolled down from the higher peaks. We were utterly alone, and yet actually we could swim ashore; complete silence, the most perfect tranquillity interrupted by the occasional splash of a jumping fish or the spontaneous outburst of chatter from the birds snuggling down for the night, followed by the calls of the cuckoo.

Awake, the air fresh, the start of the day, bright with expectation; taking the dinghy ashore, an early morning walk along the beach and over the headland to look at the weather and to gather some of the fragrant smelling wild pinks which grow in drifts among the rocks and sand.

Back onboard we carried out the usual morning chores, having first checked our anchor, hung out some washing; the last thing we expected was any company, so engrossed we were in our mundane tasks.

"Hi there, Brits." Completely taken aback, we stared at two bare shoulders and heads on the starboard stern. Looking over, we saw a large dinghy in which sat a man and woman about the same ages as ourselves. "We've come to say hello. May we come aboard? Have you some coffee?"

To say the least, we were slightly taken aback. Their voices were at least, very British, very cultured, their expressions sophisticated, a slight amused smile at the corners of their mouths. They stepped aboard, each with just a towel wrapped around their waists. I put the coffee on, hoping the towels would stay put!

"This is marvellous, isn't it Tim?" said the woman, turning to the man. She tucked in hungrily while the man held back, more in control. She laughed, introduced herself as Sandra and her partner as Tim. The man accepted coffee.

He said, "This is frightfully good of you. We have just anchored in the bay." He waved to a large white yacht, much to our relief. "I'm with, or rather was with the British Council. Yes, afraid so, a Thatcher reject, early retired." His laughter was a trifle bitter. "Well we're off fishing, stick around, come and have a drink this evening."

Later in the day we debated, we had planned actually to return to our mooring. Shall we stay out on anchor another night and accept the invite for drinks?

"Tell you what, why don't we radio over and say can we stop by early as we wish to be back in the harbour by nightfall." So this we did. Change of clothes, feeling a little more civilised, Alan turned to me and said, "Dash it all, Ann, I don't feel like getting into the dinghy and getting wet, tell you what, we're returning to our mooring and it's a perfectly calm evening, I'm going to motor across and raft up – OK with you? Right!"

As we approached the other yacht, we heard, "Well, we asked them for drinks but I didn't expect them to come alongside."

"Sh."

Tim stood on the bow, quite in command and quite unconcerned. "Sure, I'll take your line," he responded to our request to raft up.

We went alongside with buoys out and moored onto their yacht. Stepping aboard, dry and groomed. A lovely feeling at sea.

As we became acquainted with Sandra and Tim we learnt that Tim had been pensioned off at the age of fifty and had separated from his wife, had a boy still at boarding school, and a daughter about to go up to university, at which he declared, "No more fees!" Sandra had enjoyed living in Africa and had two sons there.

"In London," Tim said, "we lived on a canal boat on the Thames, within walking distance of the office, so when retirement came so early, Sandra and myself decided to buy this yacht and sail around the world. Of course, we arrived here in Porto Vecchio to go to the Post Office to collect my pension, only to find the Post Office en grieve So we will have to wait – hole up here on the anchor and hope the strike does not last too long. Like a fool I arranged for my pension through the post. What did you do, if I may ask?"

"Well, we were advised by our bank manager to have the pension paid into the bank, have an auto transfer on our accounts, in order to stay in credit and not pay charges and also have interest. We carry euro-cheques and a handful of Travellers' cheques and some currency. Always have three mixed possibilities."

Tim nodded. "I did not take into account strikes, but tonight, my love, I will make you a wonderful fish dish in wine."

Sandra laughed. "We have a well-stocked drinks cupboard and little food!"

"Forgive us, we must away, we have to be at the airport in the morning, to meet our son, but we will radio you tomorrow and come and see you."

"Oh Alan!"

"I know, Ann, but there is not a lot we can do, we will do what we can, our own resources are stretched as it is! Still, maybe this strike will be over on Monday, let's hope so."

Sunday dawned bright and sunny and found us once again racing to the airport to meet Rich.

We arrived with ten minutes to wait and wandered around the airport lounge. Not many departures. We took some seats in the cool shady part, smiling at an elegant lady who caught our eye.

"I say, would you be frightfully kind and sit with Nanny, just for a few moments, while I get the rest of the luggage?"

We glanced at Nanny, an enormous mound of trembling flesh wrapped from head to foot in black cotton, clutching her rosary beads and mumbling to herself, her eyes wild. We glanced back at Madam, questioningly, nodding assent.

"Poor Nanny, she has been with me since we lived in Africa, She is frightened in Corsica, we live by the sea and the rocks terrify her when it is stormy as it was last night in Bonifacio. She will be all right back in London. Thank you, I won't be a moment." I went and sat by Nanny and spoke slowly and clearly. "It was a horrid storm last night, none of us like the mistral when it suddenly blows."

Nanny gulped, clutching her rosary, "Yer, yer, yer."

"But it is lovely and sunny, all is calm." Nanny stared at us with big eyes, calm slowly clouding her gaze. Madam returned.

"Thank you so much, I do appreciate it. There, there Nanny, all is well." She turned to us. "Nanny has been with us since I was a baby. I just had to bring her with me even though she does not like it. She has been helping me spring clean the villa."

The sound of an engine, aeroplane engines, captured our immediate attention and we watched as the plane circled to land on the airstrip in the mountainous countryside.

Rich told us later that he held his breath and hoped the pilot got it right.

"Hi, Mum, where is she?" Still our son, as usual, only one thought, where's the boat. To his delight, within half an hour we were on board and ready to sail up the channel for that swim he had been waiting for all day. As we approached Sandra and Tim's yacht, over the radio we told them we would anchor near and invited them over for tea. Traditional Sunday afternoon tea with homemade fruit cake and cucumber sandwiches.

"Yes, we hope to make Bonifacio in the next day or so," we responded to their question. "If the strike is over maybe we can sail in company with you," said Tim.

Sandra chortled, "We don't have a chart of this area, we have many charts but there is a limit!"

After a cheerful and substantial tea and swim we returned again to our mooring, as our son had arrived without his camera and, as he wanted prints, a film would be needed for him to be able to use our camera. To our joy, next day, purchasing a film in the old town, a very elegant couple hailed us. Sandra and Tim, all smiles, waving their post.

The weather forecast made us hasten, we should have sailed by now, hoping to reach Bonifacio in a weather window. I hurried them along, anxiously watching the sky.

The object of this visit was for Richard to navigate and sail down the east coast of Corsica into Bonifacio. Leaving Porto Vecchio at eleven-thirteen a.m. the wind five to ten knots east to south east Mer Belle, but as we left the channel and turned La Chiappa point, the sea changed to a dark lumpy swell.

"It's OK, Mum, you've hung up your parsley and garlic and inspected your bilges."

"Ha, ha ha. Have you checked all your gear and your harnesses?"

A standing joke, the parsley and garlic, a reference to my Welsh origins, herbs hung up to dry to keep away evil spirits, and, of course, I never sail before looking in the bilges and checking the lifejackets. We sailed on for four and a half hours, arriving at Rondinara, the only place we could 'hole up' en route to Bonifacio. Having had our coffee and lunch whilst sailing, the decision on reaching Rondinara at three forty p.m. whether to stop for a meal and anchor overnight or carry on to Bonifacio, which would mean reaching Bonifacio seven thirty to eight p.m. A long day or stop and sail into Bonifacio bright and early in the morning. The decision was made to stop, ignoring to our cost the rule, 'sail while you may'. However, decision taken. It was a lovely evening in a delightful, well-sheltered, sandy bay, where a yacht may anchor in two or three fathom depths in firm sand. While the small cove in the northern corner of the bay, beyond a rocky spur has two fathom depths and shelter all round and a sandy beach close by. In company with three other yachts, including one of the Yacht Cruising Association, a starry night and a really beautifully calm sea, the dinner cooking: Corsican veal preceded with a chanteray melon filled with grapes and cherries, followed by chevre and camembert cheeses, accompanied with a bottle of claret.

"Come on, Mum, waltzing is all the rage. Show me how to do it." So on the stern we danced, one two three, one two three, with little room to stumble and much hilarity!

In the early hours of the morning, I awoke abruptly to see Alan's half pyjama clad figure disappearing on deck, in bare feet. Alarm! Instantly awake, I was aware of a very strong wind.

"It's OK, I'm checking the anchor."

"Dad." Richard appeared in under pants and tee-shirt, rubbing sleep from his eyes, hair tousled. He was alert very quickly, pulled on deck shoes and was up on deck in a flash. "Gee!" he let out a few choice words. After quiet consultation, they decided to put out a further anchor to hold her steady. Obviously the wind had risen and the sea splashed in angry spray as it dashed against the rocks at the entrance to the little bay.

At eleven forty a.m. we were still waiting for the wind to drop. Needless to say, nobody sailed.

The Y.C.A. crew organised a barbeque on the shore that evening, to which they kindly invited us, which helped to relieve the tedium of being 'holed in' A mistral was certainly blowing and we cursed as we realized it could be three, five or even nine days. Problems. frustrating and boring. We played bridge and just sat it out, hoping for a change the next day. Wednesday dawned, overcast and blowing like hell, to our dismay. Thursday, seven thirty a.m. check anchors, the others were setting off. "Right let's put our noses out, up anchors." Getting out of Rondinara, the swell was very heavy and harnesses were necessary. We wave bashed for an hour downwind in the direction of Bonifacio, the only point where a decision had to be taken, whether to take the Piantarella Channel, recommended only by day, in clear weather, without an east wind. The two beacons forming the leading marks for the channel are difficult to distinguish and one must follow the instructions carefully. Were it not for the very clear water, one could not detect the more important submerged rocks. A handy vessel of modest draught is recommended to navigate this area.

"We're in the Piantarella Channel now, Ann."

"What?" I rushed on deck, to watch our depth carefully, amazed that we had reached this point so quickly. "Well, we knew we could go and that it would be a fast passage and that we would run out of the heavy swell fairly soon."

"Hey, Mum, what are those shacks on the Cliffside; are they mining or something?"

Alan laughed and he responded, "Those drab wooden clad shacks were designed by an architect and it is a very select villa consortium. The design is supposed to merge into rocky landscapes."

Richard shook his head in bewilderment. "They still look like left over mining shacks to me, but they have a certain attraction. A super position for a holiday home." Richard drew his breath in sharply, "Gee, it's fantastic, quick, the camera."

"If you hold on we can go in much closer and you will get some good shots." The scene of course, Richard's first sight of Bonifacio with the crazy, tilting rows of houses, perched on the old walls of the fortified town built on the cliff side. A spectacular sight viewed from the sea.

"OK now we have to find the harbour entrance in the cliff. Richard, would like to take the wheel." His immediate and full concentration centred on navigating the entrance and of course, it was ten ten a.m. and the ferry boat emerged from the rock face. "Where did that that come from?"

"That is where we are going, slow engine and keep out of his wash."

"Ah, I see, there's the starboard buoy. GEE, this is fantastic!" The fiord like harbour opened up in front of our eyes into a natural film set. The morning was worth waiting for.

The steep, landlocked harbour emerged before our eyes, overshadowed by an impressive medieval fortress village. Ten fifty-five a.m. saw us moored up, refuelling, our first chore, as it is always a good routine procedure to refuel at the first opportunity so that one is able to take advantage of the weather and time, to set sail for departure. Then on up the harbour onto a mooring near the quay. Walking around the harbour we saw 'Sir Vagabond', a yacht from South Caernarvonshire Yacht Club, moored up, busy disentangling a very torn spinnaker, evidence of the recent winds. Another sad sight a yacht from the Y.C.A fleet which had experienced difficulties crossing from Nice, and had to be towed in with damaged hull and a broken mast. Richard viewed all this with a very serious expression on his face.

Yes. It can happen!

"But come Mum, Dad, show me the old town after lunch and to-night I'm going to take you to dine on the waterfront."

As dusk fell, the harbour took on an even more magical and fairy tale appearance. We dined leisurely and conversation naturally centred on the sailing conditions. A chuckle and a strong Australian accent, from a nearby table, let out a choice comment on the weather and all the yachties in the restaurant looked up in mutual agreement, and it naturally followed that the conversation, as everywhere in the sailing circles, flowed throughout the restaurant. Strolling back along the quay we found ourselves in company with the Australian and his girlfriend, their yacht moored near to our own. 'Joint Venture' Richard, of course, drooled over their racing machine.

The team had been racing at Napoli, as a warm up for Cowes. "We are on our way to your country for the Admiral's Cup," said Michael. We turned and returned to our boat for coffee, as it is more spacious and not stripped of comfort as is a racing yacht.

Jane, Michael's girlfriend explained, that Michael is the team manager and it is his job to deal with all the problems and get the boat to each venue. "Yes, he has headaches and it is my job to look after headaches." They exchanged intimate loving glances. Jane turned her head and continued, "Yes, well, there I was in San Francisco. I had a nice flat, cosy and content with my two cats. One evening I was invited to the local yacht club. I didn't really feel like making the effort to go, but I went and in walked this tall, dishy guy, very elegantly dressed as he had been to a wedding. Our eyes met and held, but he didn't even speak to me. Next day I received an invitation to lunch and he just looked into my eyes and asked me, if he got me a ticket, would I join him in Australia and sail around the world with him? Next day he sent a ticket to join him in Australia, where he lives and now I am here." Her eyes danced and she shook her long ginger coloured ringlets. "Last night, I slept through the storm and this morning I put my head up through the hatch and gee whizz, I woke up in Disney Land." She yawned, stretched and delicately scratched the inside of her thigh as she reached for Michael's hand and said, "Gee, honey, I must go to bed." He grinned, patted her swelling stomach. She sighed and said, "We are going to make lots of babies." He smiled and looked into her eyes with a serious look.

Early the next morning, Rich on deck waved "Goodbye' to "Joint Venture' and sighed, Goldilocks had sailed.

All too quickly we were back at the airport. A pleasant voice greeted us. "We meet again, are you returning to England?" It was the lady we had met before, when she was accompanied on that occasion by Nanny.

"No," we answered, "only Richard must return to London."

"May I introduce myself, my name is Sylvia Evans," and turning she introduced the man accompanying her, who had just arrived on the incoming flight. "William Jones." Introductions over Sylvia explained about Nanny.

The men were very quickly talking about boats and of course William was a yachtee. "No, regrettably my boat is moored on the Fowey in Cornwall."

"Regrettable?" The river Fowey is super."

"Well, it is not here in the Mediterranean at Bonifacio."

Sylvia turned to us, "Poor William, he dreams of sailing his own boat into Bonifacio."

Well, of course, after we had said our goodbyes to Richard on his departure to London, it was only natural to invite William for a day's sail on our boat, and a rare day it turned out. Superb weather and a pleasant lunch at anchor. Sylvia was very lively and active, her conversation vivacious. William, one can only describe as a 'perfect sweetie' softly-spoken, hard-working, tall, well-built, a blond chunk of manhood with a direct look in his eyes, which on occasions cloud over with slight bewilderment to shy embarrassment. Bewilderment, even at his mature years of fifty, at the behaviour of females.

He flounders, appearing to be unable to understand the frustration of the female constantly serving the male. Sylvia explained. "His mother spoilt him with love and care, waiting on his needs, choosing and serving his food, caring for his clothes, to the extent of putting clothes out to change into." In marriage, the comfortable rut of leaning on another for daily service of needs resulted in bafflement and confusion, when exhaustion resulted in rebellion and separation.

William's lips went into a firm line, a glint in his eyes. "It's to be 64/64ths this time." Referring to his boat, his alternative to a wife, to comfort his hurt feelings of desertion. He is determined that nothing will separate him from his boat, total ownership, not even shared with a loved one. No future separation, no angry partner, demanding half a hull. In his determination to build up a guard around himself one wonders if he forgets the power of the sea, advancing years, sapping strength and vitality.

A wonderful day, provoking. If only? Had we? Should we? Can't we? Life!

Chapter Three
Corsican People, Food & Flowers

Corsican people are stocky, strong, dark haired, often with piercing eyes. Their personalities have a strong reserve, slow to friendship, whilst friendly and helpful; fiercely independent, quite rightly, civilised, courteous, jealously guarding their beautiful Island. They constantly strive to keep Corsica natural, resisting commercial development, at the same time trying to maintain a Corsican economy with wine and products of Corse. A great variety of liqueurs are produced, péche, de figue, d'arbouse, de citron, de mure sauvage, de cedrat, de myrte and vin de liquer d'orange. Gourmet foods, terrine de pigeon aux chataignes, de sansonnet aux myrtes, de sanglier au porto and au figatelli. Superb cheese, Roquefort. The Roquefort Company buy all the winter milk from the sheep breeders at an assured price, thus providing the farmers with incomes.

The wines of Corsica may be described as petite country wines, making very pleasant drinking. However these wines do not travel well or keep. Each Denominazione Di Origine Controllata has its own distinctive taste; the area to the north of the island, at vin de Corse Cap Corse quite different to that of vin de Corse

Figari, which is much more full bodied, whilst the vin de Corse Porto Vecchio and the vin de Corse Cap Corse Sartens are lighter and dry. The wines of Ajaccio, vin de Corse Calvi and Patrimono are perhaps rated the highest. All are worth trying but, of course, not to be compared with the fine wines of the Medoc or Burgundy. That would do neither justice.

The scents of the island lie in the maquis, from which are gathered the herbs, the chestnuts the figs and olives. In the great chestnut forests of the Castagniccia one may go chestnut gathering, collecting on the forest floor, often having to avoid a covering of chestnuts on the

road, when driving through this region. October displays the forest in all its magnificence.

It would be unforgivable not to mention the wonderful assortments of breads made locally. Very quickly one learns that the traditional baguette goes hard within hours, hence the twice-a-day baking. However, if the pain de campagne is kept wrapped in a teacloth it does stay fresh for twenty-four hours, likewise the flute, similar to the baguette, but less crusty and much larger. The fougasse can only be likened to a large lump of dough pulled into holes, country style, whilst the margarite is in the shape of a flower and separates into rolls. All these breads are made at our favourite boulangerie at the foot of the old town, near the roundabout and just round from the delicatessen, Chez Rene.

"Ah," Rene holds his head in his hands and moans, "the mistral blows, non poulet, non canard." The wind has blown the gas out and the oven does not work. "Oui, tomorrow, poulet et canard."

Rene is stocky, plump and has a wonderful woe-begone expression, so much so that one wants to cradle his head whilst drooling over the viands, the pâtes, the poulet and canard cooking on the spit, wafting delicious aromas to the outside, way past his delicatessen. Madam is trés trés jolie, plump also, blond, with her hair gathered up on top with a red rosette. She sings softly to herself as her hands expertly assemble the paupiettes, placing a long thin slice of smoky, streaky bacon down flat, on top a long slice of fillet steak and then rolling it up, filled with their own Chez Rene stuffing, finishing by tying up with very thin string. Mouth-watering served with pommes dauphinois and green salad. Madam flutters, licks her lips, shrugs her shoulders, "Umm…, the pâté forestie, canard, foie poiver ver? And a few olives and gherkins."

But now, we must continue up to the Cave of Monsieur Imber, taking the road out of Porto Vecchio towards Bastia, on the N.198 to the village of Lecci. Soon reached, a right turn up a winding lane in the maquis, opens out into the lovely vineyard property and the cave of Monsieur Imbert. Here one tastes the wines of the Domaine de Torraccia and also buys the first pressing of the olive oil and the olives.

Chapter Four
Oriu – Bandit Hideouts

Having satisfied our hunger for interesting foods, thoughts turn in another direction. Intrigued by the stories of bandits living in hideouts, high up on the hillsides, camouflaged by densely growing entangled maquis, I would often look up and search the darkly brooding hills with my eyes, even binoculars sometimes. I wondered how young men could live and survive in the wild terrain and how such strong feelings could drive them to such a way of life. The hillsides and rocks always appear to be without any sign of movement, silent, motionless and, yet, I had actually seen in publications photographs of bandit hideouts. I wanted to search out and see for myself, if there is any truth in the stories or if they are just legends.

The area I decided to explore between Porto Vecchio and Figari are the villages of Chera and Cani. Travelling up the route to Figari, it is very easy to miss the track to Chera and Cani, so a careful watch along the route is required. Having found the turning to the lane up to the village of Chera, it is fairly narrow and one immediately feels one is right in the heart of the maquis. Chera, a tiny village of a few stone cottages, outside of one of the cottages, an old woman clad in black from head to toe, covered with a long grey apron, appeared in her doorway. I hurried over to her, fearing she may disappear inside her door. But no, she is all welcoming smiles.

"Excusez-moi, madame, bonjour." She nods and smiles. "Madam, je cherche pour the oriu." I said, showing her a sketch.

"Oui, oui." She gesticulates with her hands and waves high up in the hills, "Premier, descend à droit – straight on – Cani."

"Merci, Madame."

Going back to the car, I said, "Right Alan."

"OK, I got it."

Back down the road, hairpin right, up a dirt track. Well, it did say Cani! The track petered out into a homestead. Mmm, a waft of bread, a bakery. Children played in the sun, dogs, pigs and hens mingle around. The door to a large shed is wide open, a couple of women and a man look out. I went over to them. They were obviously very busy, as trays and trays of rolls and pastries were spread out on benches everywhere. The man wiped sweat from his brow as he slid the long handled bread holder into the oven and withdrew freshly baked bread.

Madame said, "Que voulez-vous?"

"Bonjour, Madame, je voudrais trouve l'oriu." I showed her my sketch.

She raised her eyes and looked at the man.

He shrugged, "OK",

Madame leads the way outside, the children stopped playing to stare. She waved behind a wooden hut to a path.

The man joined her, "Oui oui," he waved an arm up the hillside. Then they returned back to their bread making.

Back to the car. "Yes, I heard, and if you think I am coming up there through all that tangled, scratchy undergrowth and boulders, I'm NOT. It will take hours. OK but you go on your own, I will wait for you and make sure you get back today. In fact, it may be a good idea if I stay with the car."

So he thinks I will go a few yards up the path and not be able to take photos. I turned up the path, past the wooden hut. What a delight, flowers, soft bright green grass and on one side a little stream gently splashing down over the stones. How lovely. I wandered in an idyllic daze in the warm sunshine. The path wound gently upwards, eventually petering out and the stones became much larger and the maquis more dense.

Must remember my direction, straight up, look for identifying marks. A half broken down gate by a stagnant pond. Climb the gate or walk through the pond, the water may be polluted and full of malaria carrying mosquito, decide on tackling the gate, damn it would be half rotten. OK, torn cotton jeans. Scramble on up through the maquis, the going getting tougher. No clear path, boulders becoming increasingly bigger and the undergrowth much harsher as it scratched at my limbs.

Right. Check time, two hours since I started out on the path, I stared upwards, OK half an hour more and that would be two and a half hours and two and a half hours to return to the car. Five hours in all, I think, will have to be enough, besides one could very easily become totally lost up here, without a compass and some equipment and what about personal safety. This last factor did not worry me unduly, as tourists are usually ignored, although my curiosity was an imposition on the native inhabitants. Still, at least I was sensibly dressed, with long sleeves, jeans and strong leather on-shore footwear and, most importantly of all, no jewellery.

The going became tougher with every yard, meaning I was often scrambling on hands and knees, ever careful of the camera around my neck. Negotiating what seemed to me an extremely large and difficult boulder, I decided that is it. Sitting the other side of the boulder, scanning the horizon, one could see just boulders and more maquis for miles and miles. How dispiriting; so isolated.

Looking carefully, once more, before tackling the downward return I studied carefully an an overhanging rock. Is it? I focused the camera and zoomed in, yes, yes, a dear little house with a window. Surely, yes, they do exist. Taking my photos I felt quite elated as I sat pondering on the strength and agility of the bandits, usually the sons defending the family's honour. Family members daily climbing up through the maquis and boulders to take food to the hide-out. Defending one's family pride and honour has a very high cost.

Stumbling and scrambling down through the maquis, in jubilant satisfaction, I joyfully gathered a posy of olive twigs, rosemary and myrtle.

Chapter Five
Wait for the Wind

"You will sink, Ann." Larry, our dinner guest, spelt out in simple terms to me the vital importance of maintaining the sea-cocks. He went on to say, "Bronze are the best."

Alan turned to me, "Well, Ann, we must go to the next Earl's Court Boat Show in London and buy new sea-cocks. We will, of course, have to have her lifted out for this work." He turned to Larry. "How is the work going on your boat, will you be ready to sail by October?"

"I hope so, Alan, the work is slow. It's a question of checking all the equipment and then any new parts needed have to be found and it all takes time, especially when one is not in one's own country, although having said that with my work I have not been living at home in England for some years, although I do still keep a house up in Yorkshire."

"What is your work, Larry?"

"Well, from time to time I work for the World Health Organisation spraying crops. I've worked in Africa, a country I love, for some years. Before that, I flew a float plane, ferrying diamond prospectors across forests to the Potaro river over the eight hundred foot Kaieteur Falls in Gyana. I used the falls as a runway. For the prospectors, it was the only transport to remote areas. For me, it was the challenge. Bush flying is less predictable than airline flying, informal and one is totally dependent on oneself. I like that." He went on to add, "Yes, it's the challenge I like. So I'm now making preparations to sail up the Red Sea to Mombasa and back to Africa."

"Why?"

"L'aventure madame!"

Fortunately for us, laid-up in Porto Vecchio, excellent facilities are available for maintenance work. The following year saw Yes... But lifted out on the quayside, although this in itself was an achievement. Firstly, we found the bureau of Raffin and made enquiries regarding cost and arrangements. We then agreed on five p.m. on the following Wednesday. The young English speaking lady was in earnest conversation with a young workman. She turned to us, including the workman.

"Yes, he can lift you out on Wednesday. Do not move your boat, he will find you in the harbour." She turned to the young workman and said to us, "He is the crane driver, he wants to know where your boat is." We drew a sketch. "OK I come to you on Wednesday at five p.m."

"Thank you, what is your name please?"

"Moi, je'mappelle Jon."

Jon oozed strength and vitality, despite his slight build, although his dark penetrating gaze more than made up for this. Every inch a man of steel, even for his tender years of age.

The following Wednesday arrived, five o'clock passed and shortly afterwards Jon appeared on our bow. "I cannot lift you ce soir, I am sorry, tomorrow."

"Dans la matin?"

"Non – après midi. Deux heures et demi." He smiled and was gone.

"Thank you for coming." I called after him. He turned briefly with another smile. So, Thursday – après midi.

"Well, Ann, what shall we do? Motor over to the quay?"

"Oh I don't know, he said wait."

"Well. It's gone après-midi I'm going to motor over in readiness. OK?"

"OK we slipped our mooring and motored round to the quay and moored up in readiness, only to be met by a very angry chap.

"Not possible. Go away."

"Pardonnez-moi?"

"Your boat. No space, not possible." We stared in bewilderment. Another workman with Raffin written on his overalls quietly got on with his work of painting another boat. We turned to the angry young man, "Etes-vous Raffin?"

He looked at his fingernails while I took in his long swinging hair, a gold neck chain and gold watch. "Non," The other workman shrugged.

"Umm, there is always a problem."

"Nous attendons pour Jon."

"OK but it is not possible."

Within minutes Jon arrived and walked up to his crane, round our boat, then came up to address us.

"Can I put you along the quay. There is a problem. The other catamaran, behind you, has to be lifted out. It will not take long. Yes, just four hours. We will lift you out in six heures, OK?"

Well, we could see the problem and had little choice but to agree. "D'accord."

Three o'clock. "Well, they are all drinking, sitting around drinking beer." The large catamaran had been lifted out and high pressure washed, and had five men working on her.

"What's the problem now?"

"No electrics. The electrician is working on it, an hour's delay he reckons."

A temporary supply was connected and work continued at a cracking pace. Soon they were all using rollers to apply the anti-fouling paint. Six o'clock arrived, although we knew that a longer wait would be necessary. At seven o'clock a groaning Jon climbed onto his crane.

By the time he had slipped our mooring and fitted the lifting pads under our hulls, he was dog-tired, but we were out of the water on the eve of the French holiday, Ascension day and week-end.

Working on the public quay is rather like being at a night school class. Everyone working away on their boats. A hum of concentrated activity. Nearby, a French yacht named Tamara being prepared by her owner, a Frenchman aged seventy-eight years, for a sail to Turkey and Greece. Whilst in front of us a fisherman with his beloved Eloise, a small wooden fishing boat, both boat and owner sixty years old. Work started on the quay by eight a.m. until twelve thirty p.m. and then two-thirty p.m. until seven p.m. with the local residents appearing at seven-thirty p.m. and all day on a Saturday and Sunday.

Fortunately, the number of days one could occupy space on the quay was limited to approximately five to ten days for necessary work. I say fortunately because of the long hours. Our work on Y.B. completed, Jon lifted the boat back onto the water and we motored round onto our mooring in the marina, only to meet another problem. TAX! All yachts in whichever port would have to pay tax for that country. Dismay! We had exported our boat from the U.K. free of tax. Many yachts immediately set sail for Gibraltar. Dilemma - sleep on it. Next announcement in the port, the Royal Yachting Association stated that all yachts ten years old could apply to the Port Authority for a Declarazioni and would be free of tax. Post haste to the Port Authority. Sure enough our boat was issued with a Declarazioni and would be free of tax. Relief indeed!

Then the next day, to our astonishment we had two or three approaches asking if we would be willing to sell Y.B. Alan was deep in thought. "Ann, we could do with a new suit of sails and a new diesel engine." He went on to add, "We have done this for a decade, why not sell and buy a RTW ticket (round-the-world ticket) and see more of the world?"

This we did. Having agreed a sale, back to the Port Authority to confirm the yacht free of debt and all in order. However, as the new owner was French and planning to take Y.B. to Guadeloupe in the Caribbean, he would have to sail under the French flag. Our British flag could not be included in the sale.

Before preparing the boat to be handed over to the new owner, we had our last sail up the Porto Vecchio channel and back into the marina, and lowered our British flag.

Saying our farewells to Monsieur Lesquer, the harbour master, and friends in the port, we drove round to the ferry port to board the ferry to Marseille. On docking, we drove up the Route Napoleon to our favourite Hotel Poste, chamber dix huit, en route to Burgundy to stay as usual with M. et Mde Marlfait and to collect wine from our friends at Chambolle Musigny, dining at Ferme de Rol or Gevery Chambertin.

Endnote. Finance raised on part purchase for catamaran, with charter fees, and harbour dues, on sale of Y.B. broke even and helped with university costs.

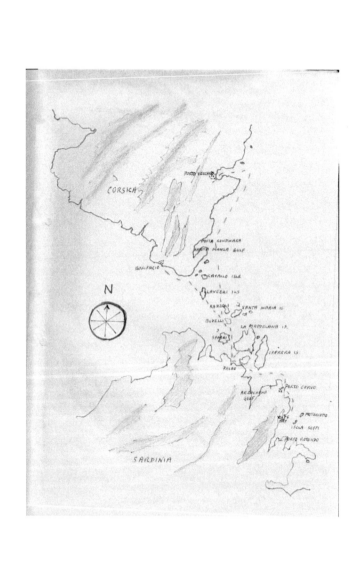

Capitaine du Port
J. L. Jesquier

© Ann Hudson

Corse du Sud

Porto Vecchio
JUNE 1988

Yes…But, 1983

Porto Cervo, May 1987

Richard helping with pool maintenance
Villa Poco Casa, Christmas 1986

Oranges and lemons in the garden
Casa Juanulloa, December 1986

Villa Juanulloa, Christmas 1986

Casa Poca Casa, December 1986

Bonifacio, May 1987

Porto Vecchio Harbour, May 1988

L'ospedale
Corsica, May 1988

Porto Vecchio, May 1988

Skipper Alan Hudson on the quay
Porto Cervo, June 1988

World Cup powerboat race – winning team – Italy
June 1988

World powerboat race
Porto Cervo, June 1988

Corse du Sud, June 1988

Chera Oriu, 1989

Chera Oriu Canni, 1989

Porto Vecchio, June 1990

Porto Vecchio, June 1990

6 knots, May 1992, Porto Veccho

Last laugh in post